Penguin Readers

CLIMATE CHANGE

HRH THE PRINCE OF WALES
TONY JUNIPER
EMILY SHUCKBURGH

ADAPTED BY HANNAH FISH
ILLUSTRATED BY RUTH PALMER
SERIES EDITOR: SORREL PITTS

PENGUIN BOOKS

UK | USA | Canada | Ireland | Australia
India | New Zealand | South Africa

Penguin Books is part of the Penguin Random House group of companies
whose addresses can be found at global.penguinrandomhouse.com.
www.penguin.co.uk www.puffin.co.uk www.ladybird.co.uk

Penguin
Random House
UK

Climate Change (A Ladybird Expert Book) first published by Michael Joseph, 2017
This Penguin Readers edition published by Penguin Books Ltd, 2019
003

Original text written by HRH The Prince of Wales, Tony Juniper and Emily Shuckburgh
Text for Penguin Readers edition adapted by Hannah Fish

Illustrated by Ruth Palmer

The Publisher would like to thank the following for the illustrative references for this book:
Cover and page 39 from photo © Robert Mulvaney; pages 4 and 47 Marshall Islands from photo © Reinhard Dirscherl/Getty Images; page 15 from photo © Wittwoophoto/Caters News; pages 25 and 76 from photo © Wang Chengyun, Xinhau/Landov/Barcroft Media; page 27 from original Ladybird illustration by John Kenney; page 29 British Antarctic Survey © BBC; page 35 from original Ladybird illustration by Frank Humphris; page 60 from original Ladybird illustration by Charles Tunnicliffe; page 64 from photo © Arnaud Bouissou-Medde/SG COP21/Flickr and Getty Images

Every effort has been made to ensure images are correctly attributed; however, if any omission or error has been made, please notify the Publisher for correction in future editions.

Printed in China

A CIP catalogue record for this book is available from the British Library

ISBN: 978-0-241-39786-2

All correspondence to
Penguin Books
Penguin Random House Children's Books
80 Strand, London WC2R 0RL

MIX
Paper from
responsible sources
FSC® C018179
FSC
www.fsc.org

Contents

New words

barrier

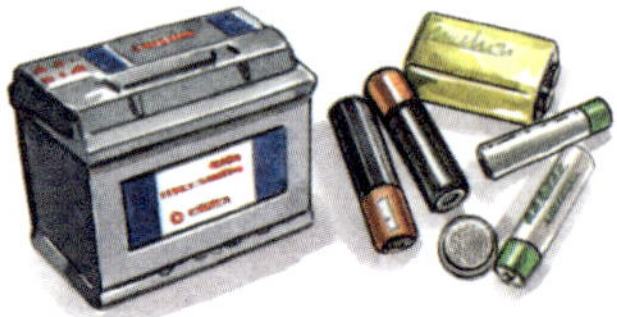

battery

buoy

flood

fossil fuels

greenhouse

ice

island

layer

ocean

polar bear

rainforest

scientist

seal

soil

volcano

Note about the book

HRH The Prince of Wales is very worried about climate change. He works with people all over the world to find ways to live that do not **damage*** the **natural** world. He first talked about the effects of a warmer world a long time ago. He decided to write this book to help people understand climate change.

Tony Juniper, CBE, is a writer. He writes about the natural world, the climate and the problems we need to find **solutions** to in today's world.

Emily Shuckburgh, OBE, is a climate scientist at the University of Cambridge and the British Antarctic Survey.

Before-reading questions

1 Look at the title and the cover of this book. What information will you find in this book, do you think?

2 What do you already know about climate change?

3 What do you think about climate change? Do you think that people should do more to stop it, or do you think that we are doing enough?

4 What information would you like to find out about climate change?

*Definitions of words in **bold** can be found in the glossary on pages 77–79.

CHAPTER ONE

The Earth's climate

Today, the Earth's climate has a huge **effect** on the daily lives of all the people in the world. It has always had a big effect on life on Earth, and it had a big effect on how life started **billions** of years ago.

So, what is climate? Climate is the usual weather in a place over a long time – normally thirty years or more. Weather can change quickly, and a place can have very different weather from one day to the next. But climate is those weather **patterns** over a long time.

On Earth, lots of things have an effect on the climate – the **atmosphere**, the oceans, the land, ice, people, plants and animals, and the light and **heat** from the Sun.

The Earth's atmosphere is a thin layer of **gases** above the Earth.

The Earth's atmosphere

Most of the atmosphere is nitrogen (N_2) and oxygen (O_2), but there are other gases in the atmosphere, too.

Some of the gases in the atmosphere are called greenhouse gases because, like the glass in a greenhouse, they keep the Earth warm. They do this by stopping some of the Sun's heat from leaving the Earth. They are very important because they help to keep the Earth at the right **temperature** for life to grow – not too hot and not too cold. Carbon dioxide (CO_2) is a very important greenhouse gas. Without the greenhouse gases, the Earth would be very, very cold.

Many scientists study the Earth's atmosphere. They do this from satellites and from the land, and their studies show that the **amount** of greenhouse gases in the atmosphere is growing. This is making the temperature on Earth get warmer, and this warming is having a big effect on the climate.

We are already seeing the effects of this all over the world. Weather patterns are changing; the water

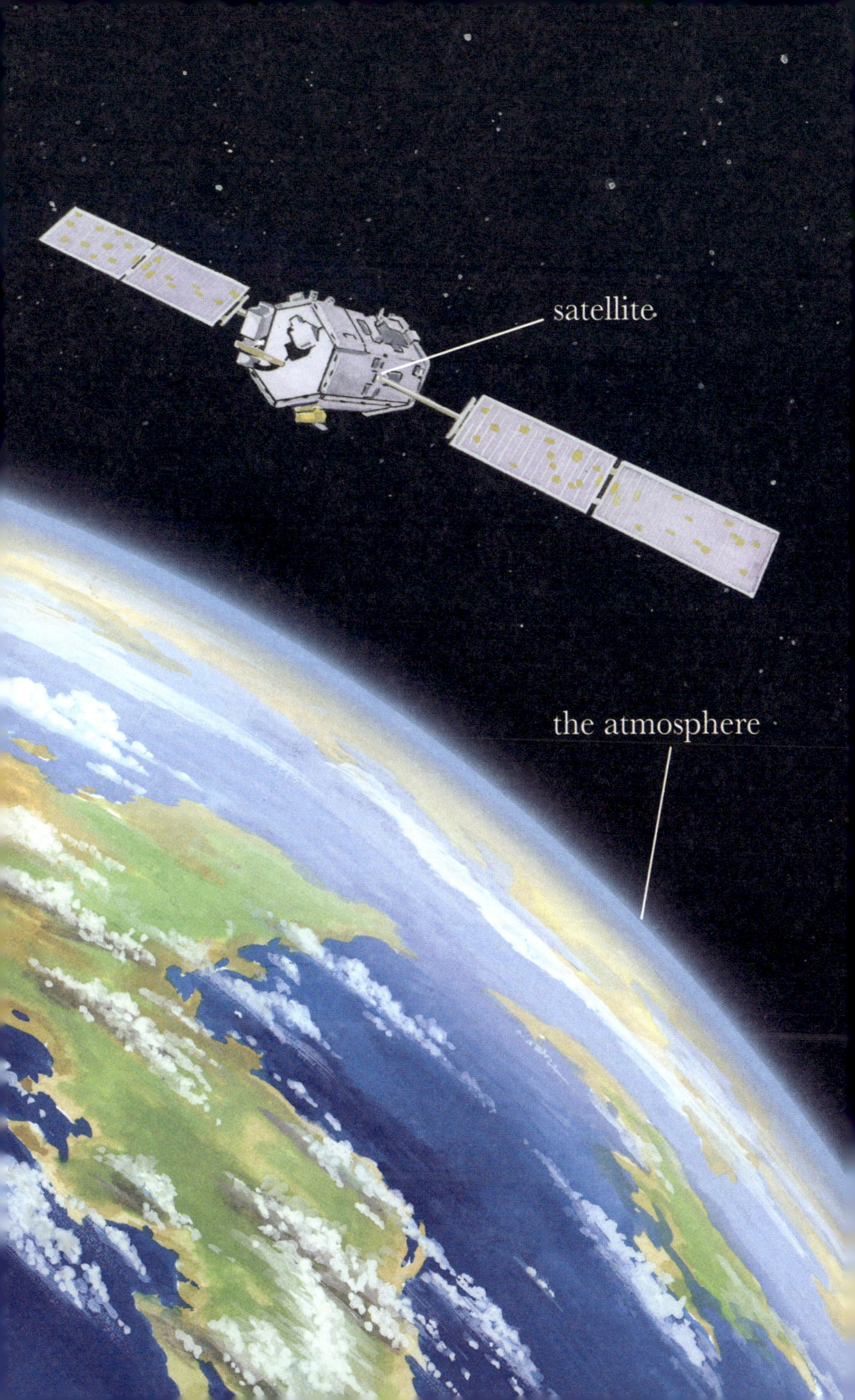
satellite
the atmosphere

in the oceans is getting warmer; snow and ice are **melting** in the Arctic and Antarctica; and sea **levels** are **increasing**.

These effects can **cause** many problems for the people on Earth, and for the beautiful plants and animals that live on Earth, too. They could mean there is not enough food and water for everyone; they could have a damaging effect on people's health; and they could make some people poorer. We need to act now to stop climate change and to make a better **future** for our world. If we do not act now, we will put the future of our world **in danger**.

CHAPTER TWO
A warmer world

Weather stations across the world give us information about the temperature on the Earth's **surface**. We also get information from ships and buoys in the oceans. All this information helps scientists to decide if the temperature on Earth is going up or going down.

Information from the last 150 years shows that the temperature on the Earth's surface has gone up. The temperature in some places has increased more than others, and the warming in the Arctic is greater than in all other places on Earth.

Some years have always been warmer or colder than others, and the Earth's climate has changed a number of times in the past. This is because **natural** things can cause the Earth's temperature to change from one year to the next, or to change over a longer time. These things **include** the amount of heat coming from the Sun, the effect of volcanoes and weather patterns like El Niño.

But, for many years, scientists have talked about climate change and the warming of the Earth. Each of the past four **decades** has been warmer than the one before.

The information we get from weather stations, ships and buoys shows that, since the year 2000, the Earth's temperature has been 0.75°C warmer than it was 150 years ago. But, in 2015, the temperature became 1°C warmer than 150 years ago. This is a big **increase**, and scientists are worried about it.

Other studies also show that the Earth is getting warmer. For example, studies show that the temperature of the oceans is increasing – from the surface, right down to the bottom of each ocean. Other studies show that the amount of snow and ice on the Earth's surface is getting smaller.

Melting ice and increasing sea levels

The warming of the Earth is causing the Arctic sea ice to melt. In 2010, at the end of the summer, the Arctic sea ice was one third smaller than at the end of the 20th **century**. That's a change of the same size as the UK, Ireland, France, Spain, Germany and Italy put together. When the Arctic sea ice melts, it can change the weather patterns in Europe, Asia and North America.

As the Earth gets warmer, the water in the oceans gets warmer, too. This makes the water expand – get larger. This makes sea levels increase. Also, the land ice in Greenland and Antarctica is melting, and this, too, causes sea levels to increase. Studies show that sea levels across the world are increasing.

When sea levels increase, floods from storms can be more dangerous for people living near the sea. Many of the world's biggest cities, like Shanghai in China, Jakarta in Indonesia and Mumbai in India, are very close to the sea. Higher sea levels put these cities in danger of floods.

The floods in New York City in 2012 showed the **damage** that big storms can do. These floods caused huge problems for the people of New York City. They **damaged** homes and other buildings, and many people had no **electricity** in their homes. This meant no heat, no light and no way to cook food or **heat** water. The damage caused by big storms can have an effect for many years and can cost billions of pounds.

For now, the Thames **Barrier** on the River Thames in London **protects** the city from floods, but, if sea levels increase, the barrier might need to be bigger. And many other cities across the world do not have anything to protect them from higher sea levels and the floods they can cause. The warming of the Earth puts all of these cities in danger. In many places, building a barrier like the Thames Barrier is either not possible or too expensive.

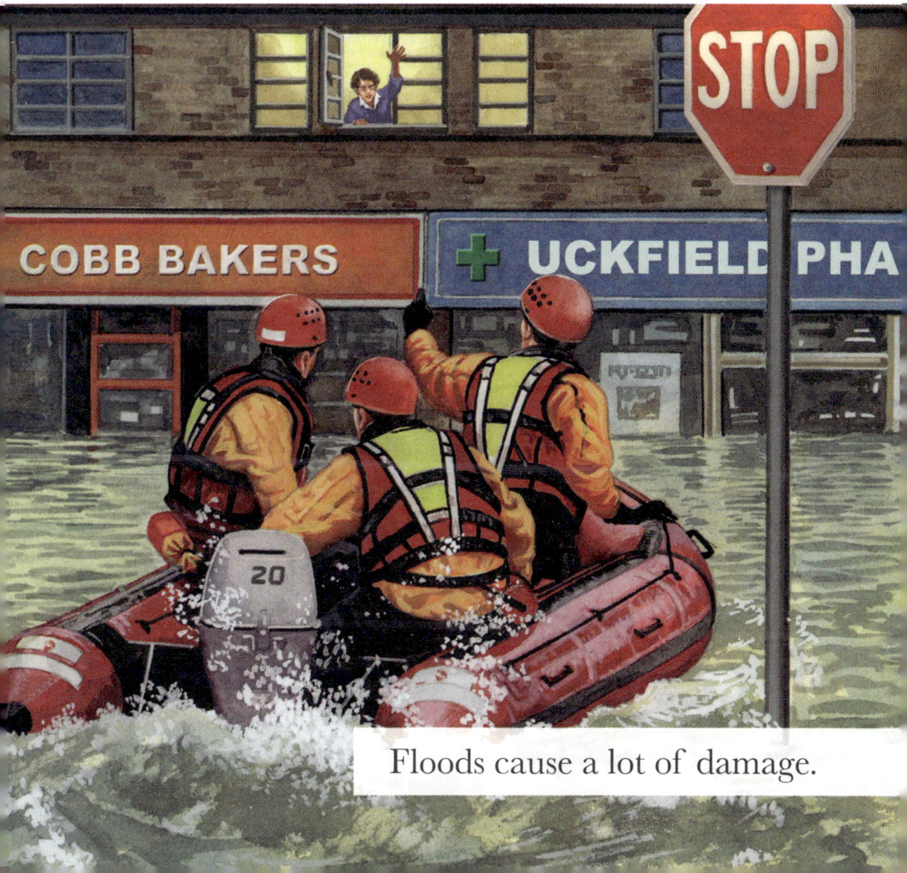

Floods cause a lot of damage.

CHAPTER THREE

The effects of a warmer world

Heatwaves, droughts, floods and storms

Heatwaves, droughts, floods and storms are all **extreme** weather. A heatwave is very hot weather for many days, and a drought is very little rain for a long time. Extreme weather can cause huge damage to buildings and roads, and to people and animals. The damage caused by extreme weather can cost billions of pounds, and many people can lose their lives.

In 2016, there was an extreme heatwave in India. The country had its highest-ever temperature at 51°C, and many people died. In Europe in 2003, there was a summer heatwave that killed tens of thousands of people. Most of these people were old, because very hot weather can cause more problems for older people.

In Australia, there have been many large fires over the last few years. In the Australian summer, the land, and the plants growing on the land, can get very dry. It is then easy for a fire to start and to become very large, very quickly. These fires badly damage people's homes and other buildings, and many people lose their lives in the fires.

Since the year 2000, parts of the UK have had floods again and again, and these floods have caused huge amounts of damage. In 2010, there were extreme floods in Pakistan. These floods had a terrible effect on 20 million people in the country. Many people lost their lives, and even more people lost their homes. It takes a huge amount of time and money to help people after damaging weather like this.

All over the world, we are seeing patterns of extreme weather. Many places are having their highest-ever temperatures, and other places are having more rain than ever before. The effects of this extreme weather are very dangerous for all the living things in our world. The number of heatwaves, droughts, floods and storms we are seeing is increasing in many places. Extreme weather is now becoming normal for many people.

There has always been extreme weather, but studies show that climate change has increased the **risk** of extreme weather. A warmer world increases the risk of Europe having a big heatwave, for example.

Studies on the floods in the UK show that the risk of extremely heavy rain is greater because of climate change, and this has made the risk of floods in this part of the world higher. One **reason** for this is because a warmer atmosphere can hold more water, so the rain is heavier and the risk of floods is greater.

The effects on people and where they live

Climate change can also have an effect on our food and water, and on our **health**.

All over the world, we grow food on farms. Much of the food we buy at supermarkets starts its life in a field or on a farm. But the food we grow needs the weather to be just right – not too hot, not too cold, not too wet and not too dry. Droughts and floods have a very damaging effect on how much food we can grow. When fields become too wet or too dry, plants cannot grow. This can increase the price of food, and then poor people cannot buy it. These people then have to go hungry. Some plants may grow better in a different climate. But scientists think that the effects of climate change will make it much harder to grow enough food for everyone.

Droughts cause plants to die.

Climate change may also have an effect on the amount of water that we have, and many places may not have the water they need. Across South Asia and China, water for drinking and farming comes from large rivers. The water in these rivers comes from rain and snow, and from ice melting high up in the Himalayan mountains. Climate change can have an effect on all of these things. This means lower amounts of water in the rivers and lower amounts of water for people to drink and use.

Climate change and extreme weather can also have a damaging effect on our health. More people could catch some **diseases** in a warmer world. Dirtier air can also damage the health of all living things.

The many effects of climate change can make people feel worried about their lives and their families. When people do not have the food and water they need, it can cause problems between groups of people and **communities**. Sometimes people move from their homes to try to find a better place to live or to find enough food and water.

The effects on animals

Climate change is causing problems for many of the animals that live on the Earth. Changes in temperature, the seasons (spring, summer, autumn and winter) and the amount of food and water animals can find all make life much more difficult for animals in different parts of the world.

When changes to the climate are slow, animals can find ways to live with the changes. But when changes to the climate happen very quickly, it is much more difficult for animals to do this. The climate change we are seeing right now is happening very quickly, and it is damaging for many of the living things on Earth. At the same time, animals are losing their habitats – the places they live. People **cut** down trees to build towns and cities and to grow food in fields. All of these things take habitats away from animals.

Together, climate change and losing habitats make life very difficult for the animals of this world. We may see some animals become **extinct** in the future because of climate change. Many animals already have problems, and there are very low numbers of some animals in today's world. More climate change may mean that these animals become extinct, and we never see them again.

Many people already know about the polar bear and the problems it now has in its habitat, the Arctic. The Arctic ice is melting. This makes catching seals to eat very difficult for polar bears, because they walk on the ice to do this.

Polar bears are not the only animals at risk from the warming of the Earth. All over the world, there are other animals that could become extinct because of climate change. Many others will find life much more difficult. Many of Australia's animals have lost their habitats because of climate change. These animals include the yellow-footed rock wallaby, the golden-shouldered parrot and Lumholtz's tree-kangaroo.

Many of our **medicines**, and all the plants and animals we use for food, come from the natural world. In the future, we may not have the large numbers of different animals and plants that we see on Earth today. This will make the world a poorer and sadder place for the people living on Earth in the future.

Lumholtz's tree-kangaroo

Golden-shouldered parrot

Yellow-footed rock wallaby

The effects on companies and communities

Some **companies** and communities are already seeing the bad effects of climate change and extreme weather.

People buy **insurance** to protect their homes if something bad happens. But it is going to become more difficult for these companies to give insurance against floods, for example. When floods happen more often, the cost of insurance increases. Insurance companies will find it more and more difficult to protect these homes because it costs so much money.

Food and water companies are also seeing the effects of droughts, floods and other extreme weather, and these effects are increasing. In 2011, there was an extreme drought in Texas, in the United States of America. Many farms could not grow food, or grass for cows, because there was no rain. The farmers lost billions of dollars because they had no food to sell.

Other companies make electricity using the water moving in rivers. But when there are lower amounts of water in these rivers, they cannot make the electricity they need. This has been a big problem for many communities in Brazil.

All of these things can make the price of insurance, food, water and **energy** go up. Doing nothing to stop climate change now may make prices higher for companies and for people in the future.

Many companies are now trying to stop climate change and the warming of the Earth. They are trying to find ways that the world can grow and **develop** without putting more carbon dioxide into the atmosphere. Together, companies are working towards a future that makes money, but does not damage the Earth.

Finding ways to live in our warmer world and to stop the temperature increasing could mean more jobs and a better future for communities.

Floods make insurance prices go up.

CHAPTER FOUR

Climate change, then and now

Climate change in the past

The Earth's climate has always changed, and this has had a huge effect on life on Earth.

Over millions of years, the climate has changed many times. It has been very, very cold, with lots of snow and ice everywhere. It has also been very, very hot, with forests of trees growing in the Arctic and Antarctica.

For the past 2.6 million years, the Earth has always had some ice in the Arctic and Antarctica. But the climate has changed in a pattern – sometimes warmer and sometimes colder. This pattern comes from the natural changes in the way the Earth moves **around** the Sun.

There have been many "Ice Ages" in the Earth's past. At these times, there was a large amount of ice over North America, Europe and Asia. The amount of ice was last at its largest about

22,000 years ago. At this time, the sea levels across the Earth were about 130 metres lower than they are today. There were fewer people in the world then, and scientists think that there were only about 130,000 people living in Europe.

Between the Ice Ages, the Earth was warmer, and there was not as much ice. At these times, the sea levels were higher, and there were different plants and animals living on the Earth.

At the end of the last Ice Age, there were fast and extreme changes in the climate that, together with people killing animals to eat, may be the reason why the woolly mammoth became extinct.

Woolly mammoth

Climate change today

Many scientists study the climate and climate change. Their studies show that people are the biggest **cause** of climate change today. Many of the things that people do increase the amount of greenhouse gases in the atmosphere, and it is these gases that are making the temperature of the Earth increase.

More greenhouse gases in the atmosphere – carbon dioxide (CO_2), methane (CH_4), nitrous oxide (N_2O) and others – mean more of the energy we get from the Sun cannot leave the Earth. This makes the Earth warmer.

Plants and animals take carbon (C) from the atmosphere. These plants and animals then die, and their bodies go into the ground. Over millions of years, the bodies of plants and animals can become fossil fuels. People then **burn** these fossil fuels in their homes, in factories, and in cars, buses and planes. When we burn fossil fuels, the carbon inside them is put back into the atmosphere as carbon dioxide.

People do many other things that put greenhouse gases into the atmosphere. Cutting down trees in forests (deforestation), growing food and keeping animals on farms, and making things in factories all increase the amount of greenhouse gases in the Earth's atmosphere.

Across the world, levels of carbon dioxide in the atmosphere are over 45% higher than in 1750. In 1750, there were about 280 parts per million. But, in June 2016, even at the Halley Research Station in Antarctica there were high levels of carbon dioxide in the atmosphere – over 400 parts per million.

Halley Research Station

CHAPTER FIVE

The causes of climate change

Carbon sinks and carbon in the atmosphere

On Earth, there is a carbon **cycle**. Carbon dioxide is a very important gas for life on Earth. Plants need it to live. They take in carbon dioxide, use the carbon to grow and then put oxygen back into the atmosphere. People and animals then take in this oxygen, use it to live and put carbon dioxide back into the atmosphere. When plants and animals die, the carbon in their bodies can go back into the atmosphere as carbon dioxide, or it can go into the ground in their bodies. The carbon dioxide on Earth moves between the land and the atmosphere, and between the ocean and the atmosphere, too.

A carbon sink is something that takes in carbon and holds it for a long time. The land and forests on Earth are huge carbon sinks because they take in a lot of carbon dioxide. This is called the land sink. The oceans also take in a lot of carbon dioxide, so they are huge carbon sinks, too. This is called the ocean sink. Together, the land sink and ocean sink take in and hold over half the carbon dioxide that people put into the atmosphere. The other half stays in the atmosphere because there is nowhere for it to go and no way for it to get out.

The carbon sinks on Earth are very important. They stop the Earth from getting even warmer.

Every year, people put about 40 billion **tonnes** of carbon dioxide into the Earth's atmosphere. Most of this carbon dioxide comes from burning fossil fuels and from factories, but some of it comes from deforestation and from changing the way we use the land.

Over the years since the last Ice Age, the Earth has become about 4°C to 5°C warmer. This warming was because of the natural changes in the way the Earth moves around the Sun. This change in temperature has had a huge effect on the Earth, its climate, and the plants and animals that live here.

If we do not stop putting so much carbon dioxide into the atmosphere, the Earth's temperature may increase by another 4°C to 5°C by the end of the 21st century. This would cause huge problems for all the living things on the Earth.

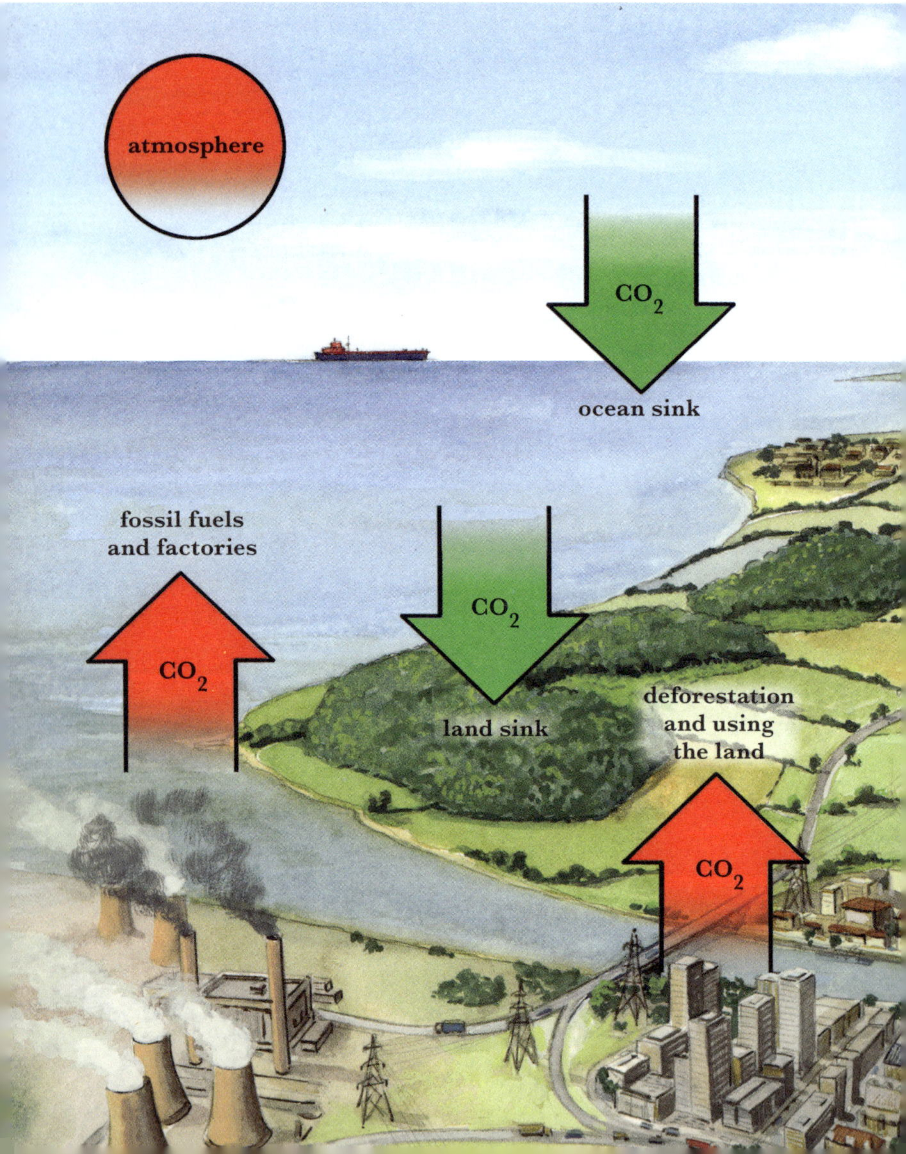

The energy we use now and in the future

Across the world, people use twenty times more energy today than they did in 1850. In this time, there has also been a change in the energy we use. In the past, we burned wood and used energy from the wind and from the water in rivers. Today, we burn a lot more fossil fuels than we did in the past. As we built more and more factories, we started to use more and more fossil fuels. We also started to drive cars and travel in planes, and this burns fossil fuels, too.

Today, 80% of the energy we use comes from fossil fuels. Energy from other things, including wood and water, is just 20% of the energy we use. Right now, energy from the Sun and from the wind is just 3% of the energy we use, but this is growing quickly. The energy we get from the Sun and wind is much better for the Earth than fossil fuels because it is clean and does not put any greenhouse gases into the atmosphere. Countries need to work hard to increase the amount of clean energy they use.

For countries around the world, getting clean energy to people at a low price is one of the biggest problems of the 21st century. As the number of people in the world grows, the amount of energy we need also grows, and this is becoming a bigger and bigger problem for everyone.

Around the world, more than 1 billion people live without electricity for heat and light in their homes. Most of these people live in Africa and Asia.

Over 3 billion people still use wood in their homes for cooking, and this can make the air inside their homes very dirty and dangerous. It can have a very bad effect on their health, and millions of people die every year because of dirty air inside their homes. Outside, fossil fuels also have a bad effect on people's health. Burning fossil fuels in factories, and in cars and buses, causes millions of people to die every year from dirty air.

Clean energy from the Sun, wind and water is the best way to give people the energy they need without having the damaging effects on people's health and on the Earth's climate.

Fossil fuels are very dirty.

Cutting down forests and damaging soils

Forests are one of the biggest carbon sinks on Earth. Across the world, forests take in carbon dioxide and hold it in their trees, plants and the soil under them. When we cut down trees, most of that carbon dioxide goes back into the atmosphere.

For thousands of years, people have cut down forests to use the land for farming. This deforestation put a lot of carbon dioxide into the atmosphere and also caused some animals to become extinct. Tarpans were wild horses and aurochs were wild cows, and both of these animals became extinct when people cut down forests in Europe, Asia and North Africa.

In the last century, the deforestation of rainforests in some parts of the world has become a big problem. Some of these rainforests are on soils that hold a huge amount of carbon. These soils have taken in the carbon slowly over thousands of years.

When people cut down the trees in these rainforests, they damage the soil under the trees, and this puts the carbon dioxide back into the atmosphere. Farming can also damage soils and put even more carbon dioxide into the atmosphere.

Deforestation

Today, people are still cutting down forests, often to build huge farms. Over the last 150 years, 25% of the carbon dioxide put into the atmosphere by people is because of deforestation.

Cutting down forests has a bad effect on the water cycle, too, and this can make droughts worse in some parts of the world. Deforestation also puts many animals and plants in danger because it takes away their habitats. It may cause many animals to become extinct in the future.

Past and present changes in carbon dioxide

The carbon dioxide levels in the atmosphere today are much higher than at any time in the last 800,000 years. We know this because many scientists work in Antarctica and study the ice there. Scientists take ice cores from the Antarctic ice and use them to find out about the Earth's climate in the past. These ice cores show that the changes in the last century are not part of Earth's natural cycles.

The ice in Antarctica has built up over hundreds of thousands of years. Over this time, snow

ice core

fell and made layers that built up to make the thick ice that we see in Antarctica today. Every time the snow fell, small amounts of air also got inside the ice and could not get out. Scientists can take ice cores from more than 3,000 metres down to find air from hundreds of thousands of years ago. By studying this air, they can find out about the atmosphere in the past.

We can also study the soil at the bottom of the ocean to find out about the Earth's atmosphere a very long time ago.

All of these studies show that carbon dioxide is going into the atmosphere more quickly now than at any time in the past 50 million years. Today's changes in carbon dioxide levels are not because of natural causes, but because of people.

Most of the carbon dioxide in the atmosphere today will be there for many years. Some will stay in the atmosphere for thousands of years. This means that we will see the effects of this carbon dioxide for many years to come.

CHAPTER SIX

The risks of climate change

Acidic oceans

The high levels of carbon dioxide in the atmosphere are having a bad effect on our oceans. Across the world, oceans are becoming more **acidic**. The last time the oceans on Earth were so acidic was about 250 million years ago. At this time, a huge number of animals became extinct.

About 30% of the carbon dioxide people put into the atmosphere goes into the oceans. This stops so much carbon dioxide staying in the atmosphere. Ocean sinks stop the temperature on Earth from getting even higher, but they also make the water in the oceans more acidic.

Scientists are starting to understand the effects that acidic water has on the animals that live in the ocean. Many of the very small animals in the ocean, like corals, are really important for other ocean animals and for people. For example, people eat a lot of fish, and these fish eat smaller fish and other small animals in the ocean. If the numbers of these smaller animals get very low because they are killed by acidic water, there will be lower numbers of bigger fish. This could then cause a problem for all the animals that live in the ocean, including those that people eat.

So, acidic oceans may cause a big problem for people, too. Lower numbers of fish and other sea animals will make life very difficult for communities that live near the sea and catch and sell them as food. It will also make food that comes from the sea more difficult to buy and more expensive.

Coral reefs are in danger

Acidic oceans and warmer seawater are both very bad for corals, and many corals are dying in oceans across the world. Storms, dirty seawater and other ocean animals also damage **coral reefs**. People are now very worried about the future of the oceans' beautiful coral reefs, including Australia's Great Barrier Reef.

A coral reef in good health

A coral reef in bad health

The risk of large climate changes

As the world gets warmer, there is a risk of large and dangerous changes to the Earth's climate. And, once these changes happen, we may never be able to go back to the climate we have today.

Even small increases in temperature can have a big effect on the thick ice over Greenland and West Antarctica. If this ice melts, it will cause sea levels to increase, maybe by many metres. This would have a huge effect on the land next to the sea all around the world.

Studies show that the ice in Greenland is melting more every summer. There is also information to show that the thick ice in West Antarctica is melting and that the damage to the ice is very large. Some scientists think we may never be able to stop this ice melting.

Changes to rain patterns can cause forests to become very dry, and this can increase the risk of fire. Fire and drought can really damage thick forests. Then the forests may become dry land, with only grass and no trees. This land cannot hold as much carbon, so more carbon stays in the atmosphere. This increases temperatures and causes more changes to rain patterns. Many people are worried that this cycle may cause many of the trees in the Amazon rainforest to die.

There are many other large changes to the climate that may happen in the future. These include huge droughts, huge changes in natural rain patterns and huge changes in the ocean. The ocean moves warm and cold water around the Earth, and this has a big effect on the climate. Changes in how this water moves can cause huge changes to the climate in different parts of the world.

Scientists are also worried about the increase in temperature in the Arctic. The Arctic holds a large amount of the greenhouse gas methane (CH_4). As the temperature increases, this methane can get into the atmosphere. This is a huge problem because methane is a much stronger greenhouse gas than carbon dioxide.

Changes to rain patterns can cause fires.

Increasing sea levels

Over the last few decades, we have seen the effects of climate change all over the world – in all places and all oceans. Climate change has had an effect both on the natural world (plants and animals) and on people and communities.

Today, the Earth's temperature is about 1°C warmer than it was 150 years ago. The warmer the world becomes, the worse the effects are for the natural world and for people, communities and companies.

Many people live on small islands around the world, and these people are very worried about the effects of climate change. Some islands are only a few metres above sea level, so floods are a huge problem for them if sea levels increase.

Many islands are in danger.

Studies show that, 400,000 years ago, the Earth was warmer, and a large part of Greenland had no ice over it for a long time. The **melting** ice caused sea levels to increase, and they became more than 6 metres higher than they are today. Scientists think that the temperature at this time was only a little warmer than the temperature today. This shows how important it is to stop the Earth's temperature increasing any more.

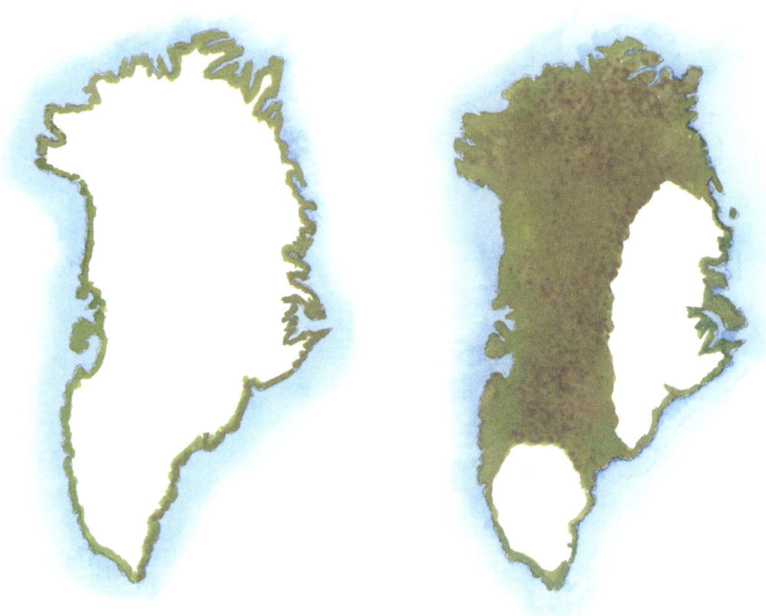

A small increase in temperature can have a huge effect on Greenland's ice.

What to do about climate change

In 2015, the world's countries met in Paris in France to talk about climate change and what to do about it. They agreed to take steps to keep the Earth's warming to well below 2°C. They agreed to try to keep warming below 1.5°C, but they know that this will be difficult. To try to do this, they agreed to cut the amount of greenhouse gases they put into the atmosphere. This was a very positive step.

These plans will help to stop the warming of the Earth and are good in many other ways. The plans could help to make the air cleaner, stop the water in the oceans becoming so acidic, and help people to live a healthy life. All of these things can have a positive effect on people's lives.

Cutting carbon

In Paris, in 2015, countries agreed to cut the amount of carbon dioxide and other greenhouse gases they put into the atmosphere. To stop the Earth's warming going above 1.5°C, people need to stop putting any carbon dioxide into the atmosphere by the middle of this century. This means that we need to cut the amount of carbon dioxide we put into the atmosphere right now.

The amount of carbon dioxide we can put into the atmosphere before there is a large risk of dangerous levels of warming is called a carbon **budget**. The more of the carbon budget we use now, the lower it will be in the future. Together, countries must plan how to use the carbon budget so that we do not use it all too quickly.

For the Earth's warming to stay below 1.5°C, the carbon budget is about 2,600 billion tonnes. But scientists think that, since 1870, we have already put 2,200 billion tonnes of carbon dioxide into the atmosphere. This means we have already used 2,200 billion tonnes of the carbon budget, and we only have about 400 billion tonnes left.

400 billion tonnes of carbon dioxide sounds like a huge amount, but right now people across the world put more than 40 billion tonnes of carbon dioxide into the atmosphere every year. We need to stop burning fossil fuels, cutting down forests and damaging soils. If we do not, we will use all of the world's carbon budget to stay below 1.5°C in the next 10–15 years.

Even if we stop putting any carbon dioxide into the atmosphere, the temperatures on Earth will stay warm, and this will cause changes to the climate for hundreds of years in the future. Because of the greenhouse gases already in the atmosphere, the oceans will slowly warm, the ice in the Arctic and Antarctica will melt, and sea levels will increase for many years to come.

CHAPTER SEVEN

Solutions

Energy solutions

To make a better future for the Earth, people all over the world need to cut the amount of greenhouse gases they put into the atmosphere. Today, we burn a huge amount of fossil fuel, and this is one of the biggest reasons why we put so much carbon dioxide into the atmosphere. We need to stop burning fossil fuels and to only use clean energy in the future.

We can get clean energy from a number of places – the wind, the Sun, plants, the water moving in rivers and the ocean, hot rocks under the ground, and other new ways of making energy. **Nuclear energy** also puts very few greenhouse gases into the atmosphere, but it is expensive.

In the future, scientists also need to find ways of making better batteries so we can keep electricity and it can be used at a later time. The batteries we use today do not hold enough electricity. Better batteries will also help us to move from cars and buses that burn fossil fuels to cars and buses that use electricity.

There is another step we can take to help to stop climate change. Scientists need to find ways of taking carbon dioxide from factories and other places that make it, and keeping it under the ground. Making new carbon sinks can help to cut the carbon dioxide going into the atmosphere.

We must also try not to use more energy than we need. We need to find ways of using a smaller amount of energy in our homes and in factories. People are now using computers to help to cut the amount of energy we use, and to put more clean energy into people's homes.

Scientists also need to find ways of taking large amounts of carbon dioxide out of the atmosphere without causing any other problems for the world. This needs to happen quickly – very quickly if we want warming to stay below 1.5°C.

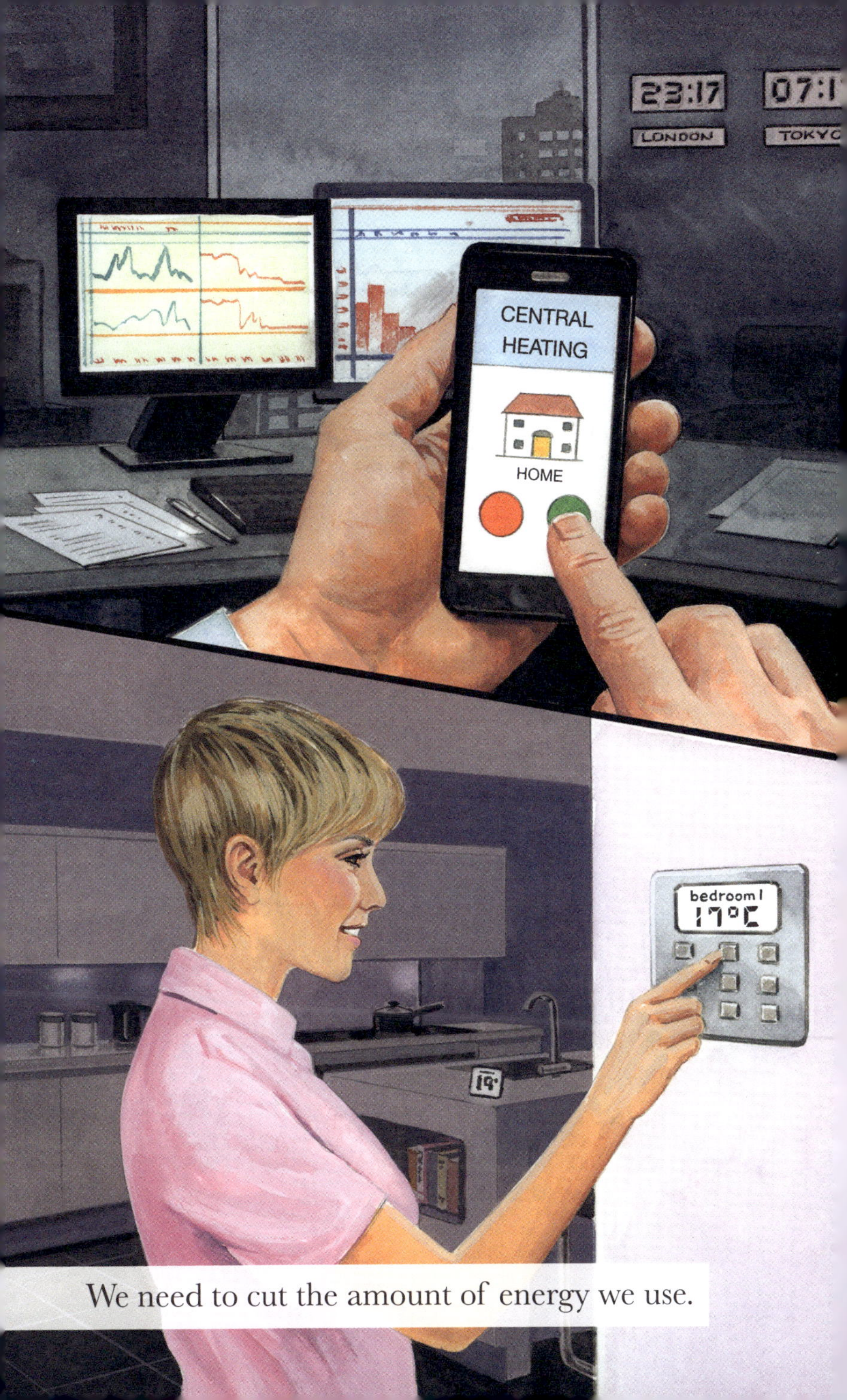

We need to cut the amount of energy we use.

Forest solutions

The Earth's forests are an important part of the **solution** to cutting greenhouse gases in the atmosphere and stopping climate change. Forests are one of the biggest carbon sinks on the Earth. We need to stop deforestation, protect the Earth's natural forests, and grow more trees and forests. This includes growing forests on land that is not good for farming.

Stopping deforestation is a very difficult thing to do. Around the world, people cut down forests to use the land for farming. This is an important way for many countries to make money and for people to make money to buy food and clothes for their families.

People need to see how important forests are because then they will stop cutting them down. This has already happened in many places around the world. Many countries now understand that their rainforests help to protect and to develop their communities.

These forests have a positive effect on the amount of rain and clean water communities have for farming and on the rivers that some companies use to make electricity. Forests also help to protect the land and soil, and to lower the number of floods communities have.

Forests do a natural job of protecting soils, and this is important for the food and water we need and use every day. Protecting forests is a good way to cut the amount of carbon dioxide we put into the atmosphere, and it has a positive effect on many other things, too.

In West Africa, people are helping **cocoa** farmers to make more money from the cocoa they grow without cutting down more trees and forests. This includes growing cocoa plants and trees together in ways that give farmers more food from the same land. Farmers are then making more money for their families and for their countries, but carbon stays inside the trees in the rainforests and does not go into the atmosphere.

A cocoa farmer in West Africa

Food and farming solutions

Farming can also be part of the solution to climate change. Farmers can use ways of farming that build up carbon levels in soils. Soils are a very important natural carbon sink.

Some soils are better than others. For example, soils that have very small living things in them can change dead plants into food for new plants to grow. This can help farmers to grow the plants we eat. These soils are also very good at holding carbon.

Farmers can help to make these good soils. They can do this by often changing the plants that they grow on their land and by not always growing the same plants. They can also help by sometimes growing plants on the land, and sometimes keeping animals on it. These two steps can help to make soils healthy.

These good soils also hold more water. This means that they can protect plants from drought, and this makes farming easier in a warmer climate.

The amount of carbon dioxide we put into the atmosphere can also be cut by thinking about the food we eat. Only growing the food we need and not throwing food away will help. Not eating so much meat and other foods that come from animals will also help to cut the greenhouse gases we put into the atmosphere.

Earth's natural cycles

The Earth and its living things run in cycles. The water cycle and the carbon cycle are very important patterns for life on Earth. Soils use the good things from dead plants to grow new plants. In natural cycles, everything is used again.

But, in today's world, people often do not do things in cycles. We make things, and then we use them. When we finish using things, we throw them away. When we throw things away, they often go into the land, the atmosphere or the oceans. We do not use them again, or get back the energy or things we used to make them.

This means that we use a lot of energy and natural things. But doing things in cycles does not use as much energy or natural things, and does not put so much carbon dioxide into the atmosphere. Companies need to do things in new and different ways. They must try to find ways of using everything again and throwing nothing away – just like natural cycles.

We need to look at the natural cycles on Earth and try to do things in the same way. Many companies are already using these ideas to make new things and to help stop climate change. For example, companies are using natural cycles to develop new fuels.

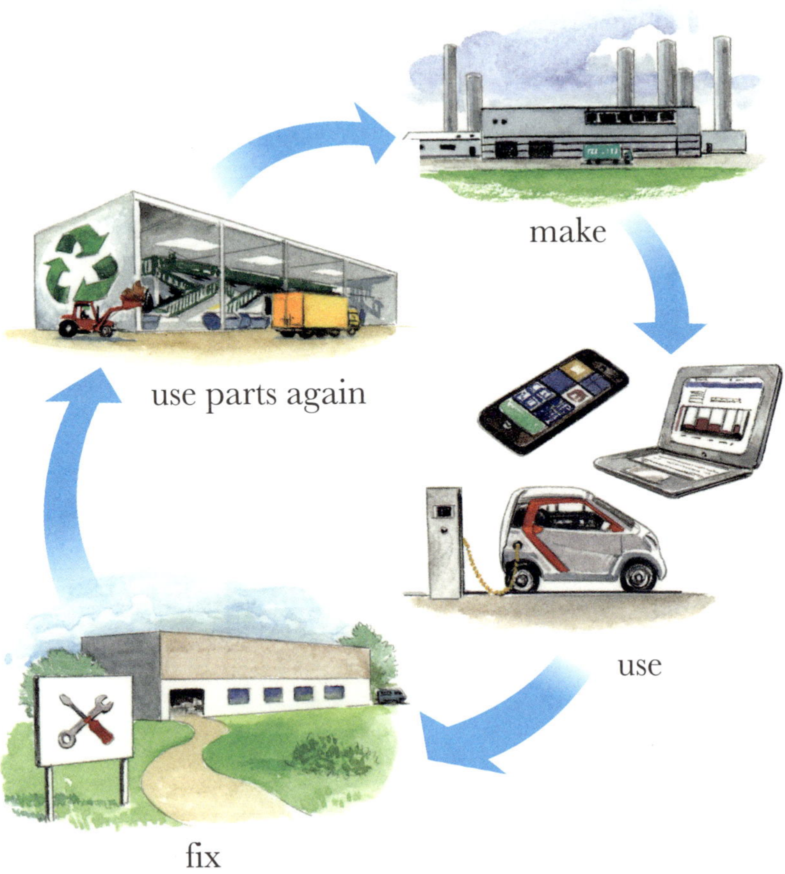

CHAPTER EIGHT
The future

Coming together to stop climate change

Climate change is a problem for all the people of the world. One country on its own cannot find the solution – all the countries of the world need to work together on this problem. Countries also need to work together to develop in a way that is good for the Earth and does not damage it. Together, they need to help poor countries and communities to have a positive future.

Many people from across the world have asked for countries to do more to stop climate change. In 2015, in Paris, countries agreed to cut the amount of fossil fuels they burn, to protect forests and to increase the health of their soils. This was a very positive day for climate change.

The steps that countries agreed to take in Paris are still not enough to stop warming going above 2°C, but the countries all agreed to do more in the future.

Countries came together in Paris, France.

Cutting the amount of greenhouse gases we put into the atmosphere will help to stop the temperature on Earth increasing more. This is very positive for the future, but many people around the world will still have to live with the effects of climate change. So, in Paris, countries also agreed to help people to find ways to live in our warmer world and to protect them from the effects of higher temperatures.

Making a better life for everyone

Trying to find solutions to the problem of climate change can be a very positive thing for many people and many companies. Across the world, companies can look for new things to make and new ways of doing things. They can work together with new people and can make new jobs. Finding solutions to climate change could make life better for people in many different ways.

Lots of companies are now developing clean energies, and this is making many new jobs. Building companies are making new houses that are comfortable, use very little energy and are cheaper to live in.

Many new homes use very little energy.

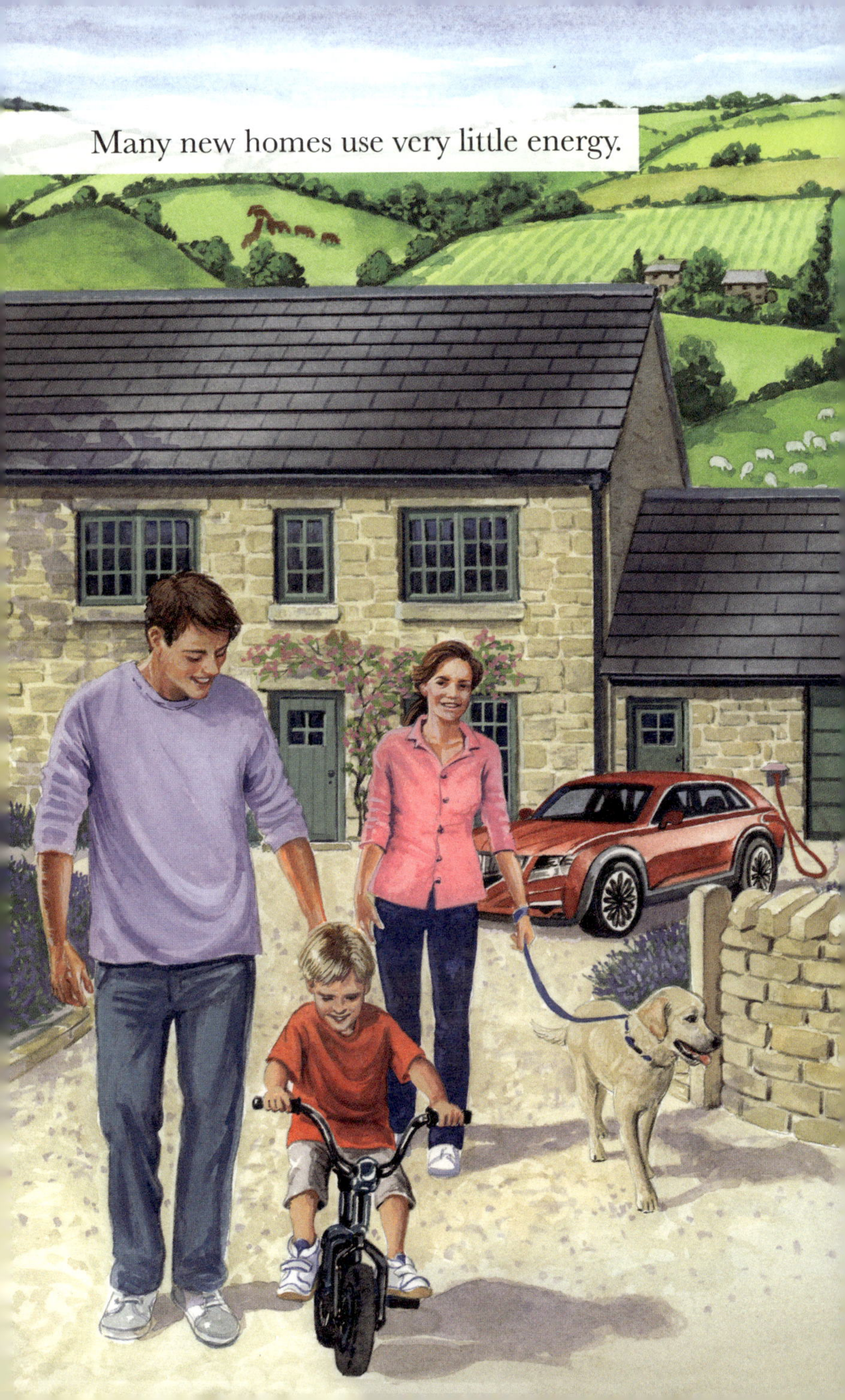

All the large car companies are now moving away from fossil fuels and are making cars that use electricity. Companies are also looking at ways of using new fuels in their cars and aeroplanes, including fuels from plants. This will cut the amount of carbon dioxide we put into the atmosphere.

A lot of companies are now working with the idea of "zero deforestation" in everything they do. People cut down trees in forests all over the world. But, in some forests, people cut down a tree and then grow a new tree – this is called zero deforestation. Companies across the world are now only using trees from forests like this.

Countries, communities and companies are trying to build a different future, without people putting greenhouse gases into the atmosphere. This idea is growing fast and is now making a lot of money. Countries can help this change happen faster – they can make it cheaper to make and use cleaner energy, and more expensive to make and use fossil fuels. Asking companies to develop clean ways of doing things can make more jobs, stronger communities and a better climate for everyone.

One Earth

For hundreds of years, we have used more and more from the natural world, but there is still only one Earth.

The number of people living on Earth grows every day, and every day we have a bigger and bigger effect on the Earth. For the communities of the world to have a positive future, we must find ways of living on the Earth without damaging it in the way we do today.

We are already seeing the bad effects of climate change, but things may be much worse for our children and our grandchildren. We need to see that the Earth is in danger and act now to find solutions.

Everyone must work towards stopping climate change – on our own and together. We can all help. Every day we can decide to do things that cut the amount of carbon dioxide we put into the atmosphere. Every day we can take positive steps to keep the natural world healthy. We have had a bad effect on the natural world for too long, and we need to stop now.

If we are good to the Earth, only then can the Earth be good to us.

During-reading questions

Write the answers to these questions in your notebook.

CHAPTER ONE

1 What is the atmosphere?
2 Why are some gases in the atmosphere called greenhouse gases?
3 What is making the temperature on Earth get warmer?

CHAPTER TWO

1 What has happened to the Earth's temperature over the last 150 years?
2 What natural things can have an effect on the Earth's temperature?
3 What protects London from floods?

CHAPTER THREE

1 What is a heatwave?
2 What is a drought?
3 Why will climate change make it harder to grow enough food?

CHAPTER FOUR

1 What has caused the Earth's climate to change in the past?
2 In what ways do people put greenhouse gases into the atmosphere?
3 Today, what is 45% higher than it was in 1750?

CHAPTER FIVE

1 What is a carbon sink?
2 How much carbon dioxide do people put into the Earth's atmosphere every year?
3 Where can we get clean energy from?

CHAPTER SIX

1 Why are the oceans on Earth becoming more acidic?
2 Why are scientists worried about the increase in temperature in the Arctic?
3 How much of the carbon budget do we have left?

CHAPTER SEVEN

1 How will better batteries help to make cars better for the Earth?
2 Why do people cut down forests?
3 How can farmers help to make better soils?

CHAPTER EIGHT

1 What is "zero deforestation"?
2 How can countries help people to use fewer fossil fuels?
3 Who can help to stop climate change?

After-reading questions

1 What is causing the Earth's climate to change much faster now than in the past?
2 Why are fast changes to the climate difficult for animals?
3 Why do we need to stop burning fossil fuels?
4 What are the big carbon sinks on Earth, and what do they do?
5 What is clean energy, and why is it important?
6 How do scientists study the atmosphere from hundreds of thousands of years ago?

Exercises

CHAPTER ONE

1 Are these sentences *true* or *false*? Write the answers in your notebook.

1 Climate is the usual weather in a place over thirty years or more. ....*true*..........
2 Only two things have an effect on the Earth's climate.
3 Most of Earth's atmosphere is carbon dioxide and oxygen.
4 The greenhouse gases are very important for life on Earth.
5 The amount of greenhouse gases in the atmosphere is growing.
6 We have not seen any effects of climate change yet.

2 In your notebook, match the words to the definitions.

Example: *1 – e*

1	amount	a	the top or outside part of something
2	temperature	b	the time after now (tomorrow, next week, next year)
3	pattern	c	how hot or cold something or someone is
4	gas	d	when something bad might happen
5	surface	e	how much there is of something
6	future	f	how something happens, again and again
7	risk	g	a thing like air that you often cannot see

CHAPTER TWO

3 Write the past participle of these verbs in your notebook.

1 go up ....*gone up*........
2 increase
3 change
4 talk
5 be

4 **Write the correct verb forms, present perfect or past simple, in your notebook.**

1 Information from the last 150 years shows that the temperature on the Earth's surface ***has gone*** / **went** up.

2 The Earth's climate **has changed** / **changed** a number of times in the past.

3 For many years, scientists **have talked** / **talked** about climate change and the warming of the Earth.

4 In 2015, the temperature **has become** / **became** 1°C warmer than 150 years ago.

5 There **has been** / **was** a big flood in New York City in 2012.

CHAPTER FOUR

5 **Complete these sentences in your notebook, using the correct word or phrase.**

1 For the past 2.6 million years, the Earth has always had some ....*ice*............. in the Arctic and Antarctica.

2 About 22,000 years ago, there was an Ice Age, and .... were about 130 metres lower than they are today.

3 Between the Ice Ages, Earth was ...., and there was not as much ice.

4 Studies show that .... are the biggest cause of climate change today.

5 The amount of .... gases in the atmosphere is increasing.

6 Over millions of years, the bodies of plants and animals can become ....

7 When we burn fossil fuels, ... is put back into the atmosphere as carbon dioxide.

CHAPTER FIVE

6 Write the correct verbs in your notebook.

1 The Earth's temperature **should** / ***may*** increase by another 4°C to 5°C by the end of the 21st century.
2 A warmer Earth **must** / **would** cause huge problems for all the living things on Earth.
3 We **must not** / **cannot** burn so many fossil fuels.
4 We **should** / **might** try to find a way to get clean energy into homes.
5 Deforestation **may** / **should** cause many animals to become extinct in the future.
6 Some of the carbon dioxide in the atmosphere today **will** / **must** stay there for thousands of years.
7 We **must** / **cannot** do something today to stop climate change.

CHAPTER SIX

7 Complete these sentences in your notebook, using the words from the box.

acidic	cut	islands	coral	risk

1 High levels of carbon dioxide are making our oceans more ....*acidic*............ .
2 Australia's Great Barrier Reef is a beautiful .... reef.
3 There is a .... of large and dangerous changes to the Earth's climate.
4 Increasing sea levels are a huge problem for people who live on ....
5 Countries agreed to .... the amount of greenhouse gases they put into the atmosphere.

CHAPTER SEVEN

8 Complete these sentences in your notebook, using the correct form of the verb in brackets.

1 People all over the world need ....*to cut*........... (cut) the amount of greenhouse gases they put into the atmosphere.
2 We need to stop .... (burn) fossil fuels.
3 We can .... (get) clean energy from a number of places.
4 We must .... (try) not to use more energy than we need.
5 People need .... (understand) how important forests are.
6 Protecting forests is a good way to stop .... (put) so much carbon dioxide into the atmosphere.
7 We should try .... (use) natural cycles when we make new things.

CHAPTERS ONE TO EIGHT

9 In your notebook, match the words to the pictures.

Example: *1 – e*

1 polar bear
2 greenhouse
3 scientist
4 fossil fuels
5 volcano

a 

b 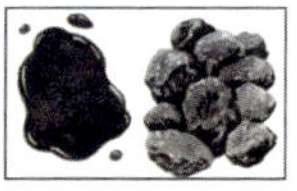

c 

d 

e 

Project work

1 Write about the main causes of climate change. What are some of the solutions in this book?

2 How can you help to stop climate change? Write a list of things you can change in your life.

3 How can you and your friends help to stop climate change? What things can you do in your town? Make a poster showing these things.

4 How can your country help to stop climate change? Write a letter to an important person in your country, and suggest some changes for them to make.

An answer key for all questions and exercises can be found at **www.penguinreaders.co.uk**

Glossary

acidic (adj)
Acidic water has acid in it. Acid can *burn* things.

amount (n)
how much there is of something

around (prep)
on every side of something

atmosphere (n)
all the Earth's *gases*

barrier (n)
A *barrier* stops things or people from moving to another place.

billion (n)
one thousand million; the number 1,000,000,000

budget (n)
a plan of how much of something you will use

burn (v)
to hurt something or make it disappear with fire or *heat*

cause (v and n)
to make something happen. Something happens because of a *cause*.

century (n)
100 years. The 20th *century* is the time between 1901 and 2000.

cocoa (n)
Cocoa is brown and makes chocolate. It comes from trees in warm countries.

community (n)
a group of people. These people all live in the same place.

company (n)
A *company* makes and sells things.

coral reef (n)
a group of *coral* (= pink or white rock) under the sea. A very small sea animal makes *coral*.

cut (v)
to make an *amount* smaller

cycle (n)
when things happen again and again in the same way

damage (v and n)
to break or hurt something. The *damage* is what something is like after this has happened.

decade (n)
ten years

develop (v)
to change and grow in different ways

disease (n)
when something is wrong with your body, and this makes you ill

effect (n)
a change that happens because of another thing

electricity (n)
Electricity makes machines work. It can make *heat* and light.

energy (n)
Electricity makes *energy*. This makes machines work. It makes *heat* and light.

extinct (adj)
If an animal is *extinct*, it does not live in the world now.

extreme (adj)
very strong or large in *amount*. *Extreme* weather is very hot, cold or wet.

future (n)
the time after now (tomorrow, next week, next year)

gas (n)
a thing like air. You often cannot see it.

health (n)
how your body feels. Good *health* is when you feel well. Bad *health* is when you feel ill.

heat (n and v)
when something feels warm or hot. If you *heat* something, you make it warm or hot.

in danger (phr)
If someone or something is *in danger*, a bad thing might happen to them.

include (v)
to have something or someone as part of a larger group

increase (v and n)
to become bigger in size or *amount*, or to make something become bigger in size or *amount*

insurance (n)
You pay money to an *insurance company*. Then they pay money to you if something bad happens to your house or if you become ill.

level (n)
the *amount* of something. The sea *level* is how high the sea is.

natural (adj)
there because of nature (= things in the world like plants, trees and animals, or the sea, land and sky) and not because of people

nuclear energy (n)
energy from breaking atoms (= very small things. Everything is made of them.)

pattern (n)
how something happens, again and again

protect (v)
to look after something or someone and stop bad things from happening to them

reason (n)
why something happens or why someone does something

risk (n)
when something bad might happen

solution (n)
an answer to a question or problem

surface (n)
the top or outside part of something

temperature (n)
how hot or cold something or someone is

tonne (n)
a way of saying how heavy something is. A *tonne* is 1000 kilograms.

weather station (n)
Weather stations have special machines that give us information about the weather.

Penguin Readers

Visit **www.penguinreaders.co.uk**
for FREE Penguin Readers resources.